Earth Magic

To the new generation: Aaron, Osei, Ayanna,
Aisha, Osaze, Dara Ayodele, Khalid, Zakiya — D.B.

For Alice Teichert and the Visual Poetry Group
because they share the journey — E.F.

KCP Poetry is an imprint of Kids Can Press

Text © 1979, 2006 Dionne Brand
Illustrations © 2006 Eugenie Fernandes

Kids Can Press acknowledges the financial support of the Government of Ontario, through
the Ontario Media Development Corporation's Ontario Book Initiative; the Ontario Arts
Council; the Canada Council for the Arts; and the Government of Canada, through the
BPIDP, for our publishing activity.

Published in Canada by   Published in the U.S. by
Kids Can Press Ltd.   Kids Can Press Ltd.
29 Birch Avenue   2250 Military Road
Toronto, ON M4V 1E2   Tonawanda, NY 14150

www.kidscanpress.com

The artwork in this book was rendered in acrylic collage on stretched canvas.
The text is set in Tempus Sans.

Edited by Tara Walker
Designed by Karen Powers
Printed and bound in China

This book is smyth sewn casebound.

CM 06 0 9 8 7 6 5 4 3 2 1

Library and Archives Canada Cataloguing in Publication

Brand, Dionne, 1953–
        Earth magic / poems by Dionne Brand ; with illustrations by Eugenie Fernandes.

Poems.

ISBN-13: 978-1-55337-706-1   ISBN-10: 1-55337-706-0

1. Children's poetry, Canadian (English). I. Fernandes, Eugenie,
1943– II. Title.

PS8553.R275E27 2005   jC811'.54   C2005-904317-2

Kids Can Press is a l,©rus™ Entertainment company

Earth Magic

Poems by Dionne Brand

With Illustrations by Eugenie Fernandes

KCP POETRY

An Imprint of Kids Can Press

Morning

Day came in
on an old brown bus
with two friends.
She crept down
an empty street
bending over
to sweep the thin dawn away.
With her broom,
she drew red streaks
in the corners
of the dusty sky
and finding a rooster still asleep,
prodded him into song.
A fisherman,
not far from the shore,
lifted his eyes, saw her coming,
and yawned.
The bus rolled by,
and the two friends caught
a glimpse of blue
as day swung around a corner
to where the sea met a road.
The sky blinked,
woke up,
and might have changed its mind,
but day had come.

Tuesday

Tuesday
light blue haze,
fat lady bug days,
in a sunlit maze.
Bruised knee spills
on San Fernando hill,
searching every street,
liking people that you meet,
step on a crack if you dare,
cross your fingers, wish in the air,
Sister says you shouldn't stray,
down that darkened alley way,
says don't stare, hurry home,
night may catch us all alone.

Tuesday fades
in a light blue haze,
taking green grasshopper leaps,
skipping down Carib street,
youth in your black shiny legs,
that mama greased herself,
in your yellow cotton dress you run,
playing hopscotch with the sun.

Crab March

On full moon nights
the horizon eats up the sea.
Blue crabs curiously
come up from their holes,
amazed, frightened,
by the wide, empty beach
they scramble and scurry
to meet the neap tide.

Fisherman

He is dark and wiry,
his bones, thin and sharp,
like the bones of the fish
in his net.
It seems as if
webbing grows on his fingers
and feet,
a starfish is his heart,
a seagull is his voice,
an oyster's pearl his eye,
he juts out of the sand
like a rock or a coral,
so long he has lived in the sea.

Market Day

Early Sunday morning,
before the sun comes up,
before the dew stops falling,
when eyelids are still shut.
We go to market laden
baskets on our heads,
walk down empty narrow streets
to the village square.
Across from the gas station,
around the round-a-bout,
down by the busy corner,
the sun begins to grin.
Then suddenly the air is filled
with myriad sounds and smells,
with laughing, bartering,
exchanging greetings,
on Sunday market day.

Eleven Years Old

I'm old enough
to work in the fields,
my grandmother says:
your limbs are young
and strong,
your mind won't rust,
we need the extra hands
to tend the crop
and feed the goats
and till this ungrateful land.

Maybe
I'll go to school
when the crop is in,
when we take the yams
from the soil,
then I'll wear a new dress,
and leave when it's early day,
for it's only one mile to the school.

13

Midday

here the sun stands
in the middle of the sky
at noon,
the almond leaves bake red,
so bright,
eyes dare not
meet the orange blaze,
the savannah is still,
the black pitch melts soft and hot,
skins, suntouched, burn,
handkerchiefs soak wet
as heat wrings water
from human vessels,
things wait,
watch the fire inch across the sky.

Drought

We're waiting for the rain,
everything is dry,
the earth and the air
and even the sky.

Rain

It finally came,
it beat on the house
it bounced on the flowers
it banged the tin roof
it rolled in the gutters
it made the street muddy
it spilled on the village
it licked all the windows
it jumped on the hill.
It stayed for two days
and then it left.

The Bottleman

"bottles! bottles!"
hear the bottleman's cry,
"empty bottles! old bottles!
bottles with corks! bottles without!"
his wheel barrow finds every rut in the street,
his sharp eyes search every spot.
there, in a ditch,
a dirty green bottle,
a treasure, a precious jewel,
an exquisite emerald in his mind.
where is he going?
from where does he come?
barrow trundling through the streets,
crying
"bottles! empty bottles"
treasures in a bottleman's dreams.

To Town

the cart rumbles
along the road,
the donkey pulling it
would rather be asleep
or chomping in some field.
we're packed in tight
we're dressed up in our best
we would rather be asleep
but excitement keeps our eyes
pinned open.
we've never been there before
only heard of its difference
from a stranger.
it's four o'clock in the morning
and we're going to town.

Old Woman

She sleeps
in a shed
with newspapers
for her pillow.
She walks
almost barefooted,
her knees are knots
that ache.
She used to work,
her fingers
too stiff now
to thread needles.
She begs a coin
her hand outstretched
"move along old woman"
they say.
She is
too old
to live
like this
I think.

Skipping Rope Song

Salt, vinegar, mustard, pepper,
If I dare,
I can do better,
who says no?
cause hens don't crow!
Salt, vinegar, mustard, pepper.

Salt, vinegar, mustard, pepper,
I wanna be great,
a hot shot lawyer,
a famous dancer,
a tough operator,
Salt, vinegar, mustard, pepper.

Salt, vinegar, mustard, pepper,
If I dare,
I can do better,
who cares from zero,
that hens don't crow.
Salt, vinegar, mustard, pepper.

Chant

In my village
blues are bluer
red are flowers
sugar is sweeter.

River

Take the clothes to the river
beat them on the stones
Sing some songs to the river
praise its deep green face
But don't go where the river meets sea
there's a fight going on.
The fight is blue and green and gold,
the current is strong and foamy
'Cause river wants to go to sea
but sea won't be her boat.

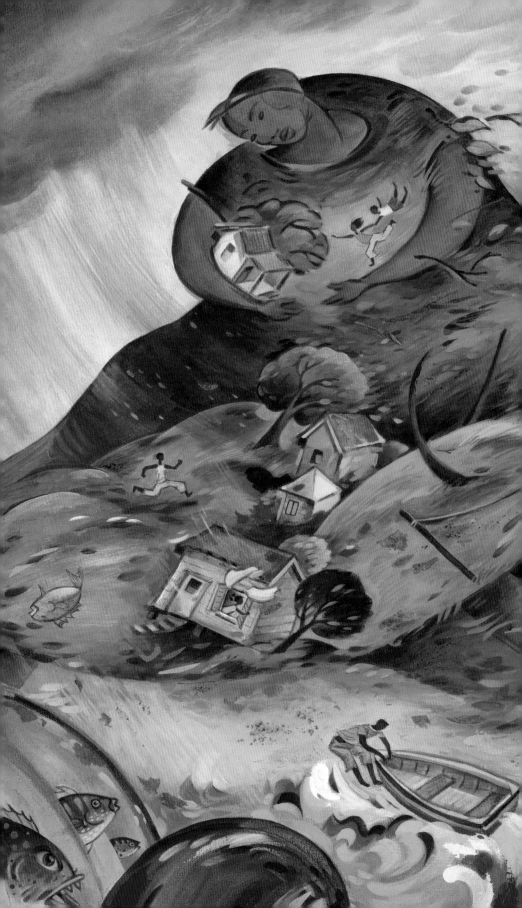

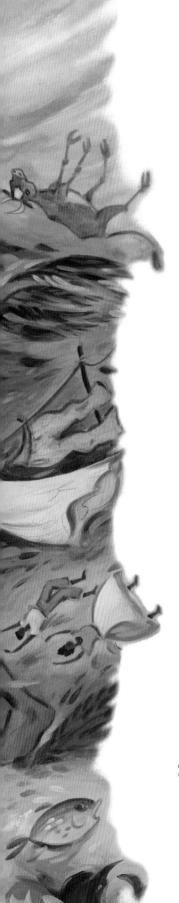

Hurricane

Shut the windows
Bolt the doors
Big rain coming
Climbing up the mountain.

Neighbors whisper
Dark clouds gather
Big rain coming
Climbing up the mountain

Gather in the clothes lines
Pull down the blinds
Big wind rising
Coming up the mountain.

Branches falling
Raindrops flying
Tree tops swaying
People running
Big wind blowing
Hurricane! on the mountain.

Old Men of Magic

Old men of magic
with beards long and aged,
speak tales on evenings,
tales so entrancing,
we sit and we listen,
to whispery secrets
about the earth and the heavens.
And late at night,
after sundown they speak
of spirits that live
in silk cotton trees,
of frightening shadows
that sneak through the dark,
and bright balls of fire
that fly in night air,
of shapes unimaginable,
we gasp and we gape,
then just as we're scared
old men of magic
wave hands rough and wrinkled
and all trace of fear disappears.

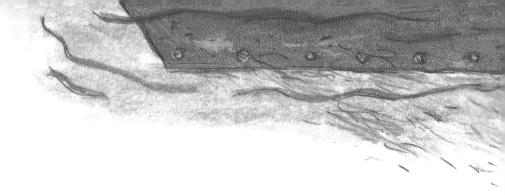

Slave Ship

an iron ship
a long cruel ship,
a ship rivetted
to an evil course,
a merciless crew,
human cargo
lashed to benches,
screams, curses,
whips, coffles,
no sight of sun
or bird or home,
a ship's dank hold,
a song to die
a mute unanswerable
question,
why?

Wind

I pulled a hummingbird out of the sky one day
but let it go,
I heard a song and carried it with me
on my cotton streamers,
I dropped it on an ocean and lifted up a wave
with my bare hands,
I made a whole canefield tremble and bend
as I ran by,
I pushed a soft cloud from here to there,
I hurried a stream along a pebbled path,
I scooped up a yard of dirt and hurled it
in the air,
I lifted a straw hat and sent it flying,
I broke a limb from a guava tree,
I became a breeze, bored and tired,
and hovered and hung and rustled and lay
where I could.

Night

The day is finished.
I see her back, moving
away from me.
I take a deep breath,
smell the salt air,
hear a grasshopper
dusting his feet
at his leafy door.
I dip my hands
into the dark water
and drink.
The day is finished.
She pulls a black sheet
after her.
She sits in the west corner,
lights an old pipe —
it is the moon.
She said to me as she passed,
"Night will keep you company
now."

Index of Poem Titles